BREAK
OUT

D1607743

BREAK OUT

A Criminal's Journey to Eternal Freedom

JED LINDSTROM

With Larry J. Leech II

DEDICATION

I want to dedicate this book to you. Yes, you the reader and your families. I wrote this book for you to be blessed in some way special so you may be touched by the Holy Spirit and set on fire to share God's good news with everyone you can.

My wife Erica and I have committed to pray daily for those who read this book. We want you to know God loves you very much. He will save you, heal you, and deliver you through whatever you're going through.

John 17:1-5 says, *"After saying all these things, Jesus looked up to heaven and said, "Father, the hour has come. Glorify your Son so he can give glory back to you. For you have given him authority over everyone. He gives eternal life to each one you have given him. And this is the way to have eternal life—to know you, the only true God, and Jesus Christ, the one you sent to earth. I brought glory to you here on earth by completing the work you gave me to do. Now, Father, bring me into the glory we shared before the world began."*

ACKNOWLEDGEMENTS

I want to acknowledge a number of people who have inspired me to write this book and encouraged me to never give up.

First I want to acknowledge my Lord and Savior Jesus Christ for saving me and setting my feet on a firm foundation.

A special thank you to Larry J. Leech II for writing this book with me and showing me how it's done. A special thank you to Daniel Strickland for helping layout and design this masterpiece from heaven.

Thank you to my good friend Russell Holloway for putting the bug in my ear to write a book and follow through with it to the end.

Thank you to my mom Donna Lindstrom for always praying with fervency and faithfulness for the Lord's delivering hand to break out in my life. I want to honor my dad Clint Lindstrom. Even though we have no relationship, I want him to know God loves him very much and one day our paths will cross again.

Thank you to my brothers Chris Warmbold and Hans Lindstrom for walking by my side through tough times and always seeing the best in me.

I want to recognize my best friend, since I was three years old, Tom Anderson for believing in me and supporting me through my addictions and struggles; Pastor Clarence St. John, a great man of God, for dedicating me to the Lord when I was one and standing with in support of God's call upon my life; and evangelist Jacob Damkani for delivering the gospel to me all the way from Tel Aviv Israel while I was still a thief and a drug addict.

Thank you to all the police officers who arrested me and the corrections officers who watched over me while I was incarcerated. Thank you to our U.S. military who serve this nation. Thank you to the Minnesota Adult and Teen Challenge leadership and staff for your dedication to Jesus and to the broken and hurting. Thank you to pastors Jeff and Vicki Dye for telling me like it is, and Pastor Rich Scherber for telling me to not mess it up again and that I could be a world changer.

Thank you to all on our ministry staff, board of directors, and prayer and financial partners for standing with us in the ministry and investing your resources.

A special thank you to our very own Intercessory prayer coordinator Pat Anderson for mobilizing people to pray over every aspect of this project and agreeing with us that Gods Love would prevail in the readers' lives.

Rosella, Annabelle and Lydia—my wonderful children—you inspired me to write this book. For this I am humbled and blessed, thank you for being a part of my life and my family.

Last, but not least, I want to honor my beautiful wife Erica Lindstrom for always loving me. Always seeing what I cannot see and for keeping me in line.

TABLE OF CONTENTS

Chapter 1

MY NEW LIFE

I watched the man approach our tent. I've seen that walk before. The one that switches from hope to uncertainty with each step. Looking tired and unsure, he stopped a few feet away and surveyed his surroundings. I could tell he wanted to come in, but something held him back.

I stepped outside, into the heat, with a bottle of water in my hand. "Thirsty?" I said over the sound of a car zipping past us on South Ridgewood Avenue in Daytona Beach, Florida.

He looked in my direction, still not sure what to do next. He ran a dirty hand through unwashed hair.

"Mighty hot out here today. Unusual for this time of the year."

"Yeah, it is."

I handed him the bottle of water and this time he took it. "Shouldn't be this hot in February."

"Not much we can do about it, though. It is what it is." He twisted off the cap and took a sip.

"So what brings you to this part of town?"

He looked around before answering, like he was unsure that he should tell me. "I've been camping with a buddy of mine." He nodded in the direction of the campground. "We've been drinking and doing drugs for the last two days. He's passed out right now. I needed to get away." I nodded while he continued. "I'm tired of being hung over and strung out. I'm sick of it. The booze. The drugs. The women. All of it. So I decided to take a walk and here I am." He dragged the toe of his boot on the sidewalk.

"Well, I'm glad you stopped by. You're welcome to come inside if you want. This heat is a bit much," I said as a loud motorcycle drowned out my last few words.

His eyes widened. "Did you say you're the heat?"

"No," I said, chuckling and laying a hand on his shoulder. "I'm not the heat. It's hot out here. Let's go inside and chat."

He eyed the banner across the top of our tent. "I've heard of you guys. You guys help people, right?"

"Well, I guess you can call it that. We just love on people and share the gospel of Christ."

He nodded, but didn't take a step toward the tent. A local delivery truck chugged by, the driving grinding a gear trying to stop at the light nearby. "I've heard about your Jesus. But I'm not sure what to make of him." This time the man took a long drink, almost finishing the bottle. "I've done too much stuff for him to even care about me."

"Oh, I'm not so sure about that," I said. "You have no idea what I've done in my life."

He scoffed. "You? You probably grew up in the church. One of them holy rollers all your life."

"That's the furthest thing from the truth."

"Sure. Look at you. How could you ever understand what I've been through? You're all cleaned up. With a world class smile. Nice clothes and shoes."

I gave him a quick once over before answering, not to judge, but to understand why he made the comment about my clothes and being clean. I could see why the nice clothes and shoes stood out to this guy. But I wasn't dressed much differently than him. We both wore jeans, although his were covered with patches of grease and dirt. We both wore T-shirts. His promoted a popular motorcycle brand. Mine was plain white. He wore a beat up pair of cowboy boots and I wore somewhat new sneakers.

"God cleans us up when we turn our life over to him, no matter how dirty we are."

He gave me a look—a suspicious bloodshot squint with the lips pursed—that I've seen numerous times over the years since giving up drugs and alcohol for a life dedicated to Jesus Christ. I probably gave that same look to people back in the day when I lived on a steady diet of chemicals and booze. "What do you know about Jesus cleaning you up? You can't know what's it like to be hooked on drugs, booze, or both."

"Why don't we step inside and I'll share my story with you. I bet you'll be surprised."

He looked at his empty water bottle and agreed. We stepped under the cover and he asked for more water. I reached into the cooler near the entrance, pulled another bottle from the ice, and handed it to him. When he finished chugging that one down, I motioned to a pair of metal chairs off to the side, away from everyone else. He nodded and followed me.

Before we reached the seats, he asked, "You were messed up on booze?"

"Drugs too." I said, taking the seat on the left so I could see the entrance. He flipped the other chair around and leaned on the back.

"I just don't picture you being a user."

"Well," I said, putting my elbows on my knees, "let me tell you my story and you can decide for yourself."

Chapter 2

HOOKED AT A YOUNG AGE

My slide into drugs and alcohol and criminal activity started at age thirteen. I know I was young, getting into illegal activities at an age when most boys want to hang out with great friends and for their dad to still be their hero. But I grew up fast and soon found myself acting and living like I was much older.

Before the proverbial wheels came off, my family was active in the church and we enjoyed a number of fun family activities. I can remember attending the air show with my dad, canoeing on the St. Croix River, fishing at Lake O'Brien, and camping around Minnesota.

Mom and Dad were recovering addicts and we attended church three days a week—Wednesday, Friday, and Sunday. In many ways you could say we were the typical churchgoing family—loving, friendly, compassionate. We hosted Bible studies, movie nights, and dinner parties for church friends. But when the church family wasn't around, things got uncomfortable.

Mom and Dad fought. A lot. This confused me. I didn't understand how we could appear holy when others were around, but not when our church friends were not. Most of the time, I didn't understand why my parents fought. When the yelling started, I'd retreat to my room. Their fights sounded like a gong blasting in my ear. I wanted them to stop. I wanted a happy family.

I cannot remember many times when I felt loved or encouraged by my father. My mom really did show that she loved us. I could see it in her daily struggle to be a woman of God with a man who claimed the same faith but showed no love through his actions. My dad's behavior tainted my view of what a true Christian should be, or at least what I thought it should look like.

My mom battled to live out her faith because of my father's tyrant-like behavior. Everyone in the home suffered. He wasn't a nice man. I remember Mom praying when he worked or was away from the house. She knew we weren't safe with him around.

The more I observed, the less I wanted what they preached at church and what my parents wanted for me. Too much hypocrisy, especially from my dad. I thought, if that's the way church people live, I could live that way anywhere. I could go hang out with the people they're telling me not to hang out with and probably have a better time. If the God who we worshiped in church was as unbalanced and dysfunctional as our family was at this point, I wanted nothing to do with that God.

I am sure my parents did their best to work out their differences. My dad hurt us with his unpredictable anger and rage. He attempted to offset that bad behavior by doing nice things for us, another example of the hypocrisy that we lived with. He left us when I was about nine. He'd been involved in some pretty serious things—stalking and terrorist threats for years—that finally caught up with him. He denied the charges, but investigators provided undeniable evidence. Later, as an adult, I learned more about his past and his unwillingness to humble himself. That hurt me for years because I hoped he would come around and be the dad I always wanted.

When my mom told me Dad was gone, I wanted to celebrate. No kidding. As a kid you want your dad to protect you and the family. You want him to be the hero, to show love and be an example of how a godly man should live. For us, though, when he left, I knew I wouldn't miss him. The loud gong noises disappeared. The fear dissipated. The pain eased.

I can't even say that I loved my dad at that time. I wish that weren't true. But I had shut him out and hated him. God has since healed me and I've forgiven him. After I became a Christian, I needed to work through some things to understand him during that part of my life.

When my dad left, we lived in fear for a while because of what he had done. Then one day after he got out of jail, he picked me up illegally from a basketball game and took me to a restaurant. He was supposed to have permission to see me. I found out later that he didn't. He and my grandmother wanted to know where I wanted to live.

The decision was easy. As much as I wanted to live with him, as any boy who wants to be around their dad, I knew being with him wouldn't work. I still saw the hateful, angry man who was married to my mom. He wasn't that way all the time, but those emotions are what I remembered the most. I didn't want to be around that. Because of his anger and sports, I picked my mom over him.

I had just been accepted to play basketball on a private Catholic school team. At the time I played a lot of baseball and basketball. If I went to live with my dad, I would have lost this opportunity to play basketball. Being on this team was pretty important to me. So I picked Mom.

Raising three boys and trying to dig us out of the hole my dad put us in with his foolish living kept Mom plenty busy. She wasn't stable at the time, as one might expect after living in a tumultuous marriage for thirteen years. She slid backwards in her faith and disengaged from her friends. We quit attending church. We turned our backs on God and transitioned into survival mode. On the outside, things didn't look bad. She was hurting, though, and pushed through despite our troubles. She did the best she could, but we still ended up on welfare and lived in government housing.

I loved sports and I wanted to be out there playing, but I knew I needed to help my mother around the house. I stepped up to be the dad for a little bit. That's not right, though. A ten-year-old needs his dad.

My older half-brother Chris, three years my senior, spent a lot of time up north with his father. He saw the dysfunction in the family so he worked a lot and hung out with his friends. Then he joined the military at an early age. I guess he wanted to get away and do something good with his life. I can't say that I blame him. He made out very well for him and his family.

This is about the time I started going downhill. It wasn't a conscious effort to slide into trouble. Mom worked a lot and battled her own demons. I wanted attention and started having behavioral issues at school. Every day one of my teachers sent me to the principal's office. I spent so much time there or in his assistant's office that they created a spare room for me. It was that bad. Starting in first grade, I was kicked out of just about every class.

One of my elementary school teachers talked with my mom and recommended I be put on medication. Mom wondered why it was necessary. She felt I should be challenged more, not medicated. Not knowing where to turn for help, Mom allowed the school to send me to the University of Minnesota where a number of kids my age were being tested. I also attended an anger management group and groups for family relationships.

In some of the groups I remember opening up and feeling better. I was very lost and confused. Looking back it's easy to see that hurt and pain caused disruptive and erratic behavior in school. I was a young man, full of fear and anger. I didn't want to change either.

As strange as it may sound, I maintained control of my life in this state. I didn't want to lose that, even though my life was a disaster. At least I thought I had control of my life. I had learned how to manipulate my way through life. So I put on a "false" face and told people what they wanted to hear.

While at the University of Minnesota, I was diagnosed with ADHD and Turrets Syndrome. Doctors prescribed a number of drugs, including Lithium, Neurontin. Paxil, Ritalin, Adderall, Wellbutrin, Xanax and about eight others that I can't remember. Over the course of my treatment, none helped my conditions. After a while, doctors were puzzled as to what to give me. I took the meds for about ten years. Although none of them completely worked, they did help me escape reality. The doctors couldn't find one, or a combination, that completely healed me. Some worked to a certain degree, but I never got total relief. I eventually began to abuse them, which led me to using street drugs. In 2001, I took myself off the drugs. If the meds weren't working, I figured why bother.

My dream back then, like most kids my age, was to play professional baseball or make it to the National Football League. I loved the Vikings and Twins, who won a championship in 1987 when I was just six years old. I wanted to be the next Robert Smith or Kirby Puckett. I fantasized about scoring the winning touchdown for the Vikings in the Super Bowl or hitting the World Series-clinching homer for the Twins.

Until one day when walking home from a baseball practice with my cleats slung over one shoulder and my glove tucked under my arm.

Chapter 3

PULLED INTO THE ABYSS

One day while coming home from a ball game, I looked over at this apartment where people were known to deal drugs, get high, and where boys and girls often engaged in stuff that they shouldn't. I was friends with some of them, but never indulged. Most of the time I ignored this place and the people who went there. If a buddy said he was headed there, I went in a different direction and found something else to do.

This day, however, I didn't turn away or find something else to do. Up until now, I had been protecting myself from that stuff and the people who indulged in illegal activities. I had been holding onto the dream of playing professional sports. I was pretty good at baseball. Even though I was a left-hander, my coaches often put me at positions typically reserved for right-handers, such as shortstop or second base. I was a very good wrestler and point guard in basketball. I wasn't the greatest at football, but I played, usually safety or corner. I loved hockey, but we couldn't afford for me to play. It's an expensive sport.

But that day walking past that apartment, I laid down my dreams to play professional sports. I saw a couple of my friends hanging out in this apartment. I thought I'd give it a shot and see what happened. I walked over and hung out with my buddies. Everything changed for me that day. We got high. I don't remember on what.

The first time I got high, I lied to my mom about staying a friend's house. Instead, I went with some other guys and got baked on marijuana at one of their homes. It was the middle of winter. While high, I wandered outside and passed out. One of my friends found me later with my head buried in a snow bank. I remember my head being numb. So, the first time I got high, I almost died. I was fourteen.

After that, if I wasn't playing ball, I was

getting high and partying. I still loved to play ball. I often went into the city to make phone calls, knock on doors to get people to play pickup games. As a kid, that was my first priority, which was a lot healthier than the whole drug thing. Splitting time between my two favorites pastimes eventually became too much to handle. My performance on the field deteriorated. I eventually stopped playing so I could focus on getting high.

My mom knew I was starting to get into trouble. She took away privileges. She sat me down and explained the dangers of life. I didn't listen. The rebellion and promiscuity kicked in. She grounded me numerous times, but at night I'd climb out my window to hang out with friends. No matter how loving or caring she was, nothing worked.

My heart was hardened, I had so much hurt and hatred built up that I didn't have any love any longer. I was still going to school, but I was running around on the streets where I started to get involved in heavier drugs—cocaine, pills, and crystal meth. I supplied my habits by stealing and dealing to other youths and adults. I became a hardcore thief. I broke into homes, businesses, stole guns and sold them to gang members. I stole jewelry, cash, you name it. Just like when I played sports, I dove all in. I don't do anything halfway.

I started to sell drugs to the young and old, rich and poor, families. I wasn't partial to anyone. One minute I would sell to a homeless guy and half an hour later I'd be in a million dollar home selling to a mom and a dad.

At fifteen, I felt like I owned the world. You pretty much could say that I was running a business. We had a crew of guys who worked together with the reputation that you didn't mess with us. Our small crew was "down for whatever" or we were "willing to lay our life down" for one another. We were the type of crew that if someone messed with us, we'd retaliate through robbery, burglary, giving someone drugs were laced with something, or might hurt them or their families. You just didn't mess with us. We were tight and we had money—a lethal combination.

I had more money than I ever thought I would have. While I dealt drugs, I also worked part-time. It was an exciting time for me. I was getting high every day and selling out of the company where I worked. Crazy thing is, I never got caught. Not once. Not even at school.

At this point, the only reason I attended school was to sell drugs. The administrators knew I was an addict and was dealing hard core drugs. But I never got busted. I don't think I really cared if I got busted. I was like, come and get me. That's how it was, my mindset back then.

Most people think druggies are stupid. We're not. A druggie must be pretty sophisticated. That's how I could stay ahead of my teachers. They never caught me with drugs and they couldn't kick me out of school because I was coming every day.

People wondered, with my background, how could I have gotten my diploma. It's only by God's grace that I graduated. One teacher in particular went out of her way to help me. I'm not sure why. I think she may have seen something in me. I'm not sure what that would have been. I was voted by my class as the most likely to spend the rest of life in prison. I think most of my teachers from back then would be shocked to see how different I am today.

But somehow I managed. I wasn't one of those guys who liked to sit home all day and get high. I was more independent and driven. While some sat home and got high, I was a runner. I still got high, but didn't spend every minute of every day getting messed up. I liked making money too much.

Some days I would do ten to twelve deals by 5:00 p.m. Then I'd go to work. On days like that, I'd get up and get high right away, whether I was home or crashed at someone else's place. Then I'd meet the guys who drove in from the city to supply what we needed to deal that day. We'd take care of any business we had, such as selling them a gun, maybe a well-conditioned 9mm with a clip for $100 to $150.

I look back now and realize the craziness, especially at a young age. Sometimes I'd carry around thousands of dollars. What I didn't carry, I'd stash it in different places. My brother, who followed in my footsteps, ripped me off a few times. I carried at times, usually the guns I stole. I also carried brass knuckles, large knives, and the like. I was a little paranoid. I slept many nights with a weapon under my pillow. We believed that we were safe, but if you know the street life, you know your life can change in a heartbeat. We were very protective of each other. If I wasn't safe, the other guys weren't safe. So they made sure I was safe too.

After I bought coke, marijuana, pills, whatever, from the guys in the city, we'd get it ready to sell. My phone would blow up all morning from people who wanted drugs. I sold to kids eleven or twelve years old, sometimes buying for their parents. I know that doesn't sound like it's possible, but it really is. I also sold to people sixty or seventy years old. I didn't care. Now I have remorse. Back then, I didn't. It's not something that you think about when you're pushing dope in the streets or throughout a community. You're just thinking about the money, the next deal, the street cred you're building.

Despite pushing that much dope and making that kind of money, we never joined a gang. We could have. We had enough interactions with a number of them that it would have been easy to join forces with one. With just a handful of us, we'd meet and make decisions together, although I had a lot of influence. But I didn't have the kind of influence that guys would blindly follow me wherever I went. I was a drug addict and criminal. So it's easy to understand that we only trusted each other to a "certain point."

Everything we did revolved around the drugs, the women, the parties—that whole culture. We didn't really need a leader. We all wanted the same thing. To belong. That was our biggest deal. We all were hurting people. And it's true what is said about hurting people hurt people. We didn't care. We were hurting people and ruining people's lives and families. Later, it wears on you, but at the time, when you're in it, your heart is hardened and you just don't care who is in the way.

We didn't even worry when someone pulled a gun on us. That happens more than people know. I remember every one of them. The first time was when I was fifteen. Me and two buddies were set up. We showed up to make a deal. The other guys pulled a gun and put it to my head. They took everything—drugs, money, and jewelry. Our first thought was to retaliate. But we couldn't. They were bigger. In that situation, a person must focus on how to cover the stolen drugs and money. Whenever we got "jacked" like that, we recouped our losses by targeting innocent people for money or set up other dealers who were more vulnerable and weak.

Certainly not a glamorous lifestyle, but that's how one survives—taking and being taken from. It's a vicious cycle. We never killed anyone, but people often die during these "transactions."

Mom found my drugs a few times. Mounds of it, actually. But she never got rid of it. Because she was a former addict, she knew the consequences if she did. I'd been in big trouble with my dealers. Instead, she confronted me. We argued with lots of yelling, slamming doors, lashing out. Sometimes she would show up and try to catch my buddies and I doing something wrong. That didn't embarrass me like you think it might. In that lifestyle people know there are families that aren't happy. By the time I was fifteen, I only stayed home half the time anyway. The other nights I'd stay with a friend or just roam the streets all night. Either with my buddies or someone I just met, we looked for valuables to steal, houses to break into, and cars to steal, anything we could turn into money. When you get more money, you buy more dope. This expands your circle of friends. At restaurants, we stole tips from tables to pay for our meal, or left without paying. I wasn't a big-time crook, but I was climbing the ladder.

I might have been physically safe, but my spirit, which I wasn't worried about at the time, wasn't.

JED LINDSTROM

Chapter 4

FROM BAD TO WORSE

Life took a turn for the worse after I graduated from high school in 1998. When you're in that lifestyle you don't think, or worry, about things going from bad to worse. But they do. And then they get worse again. A person has to hit bottom before they bounce back. At this point, I was far from my bottom. So I had plenty of room to fall.

After graduation, my mom kept her promise that she'd kick me out of the house if I didn't get my act together. I didn't care. I packed a black garbage bag full of my clothes and moved in with my girlfriends' friends who liked to party. I was a street runner at the time so I was comfortable on the streets. Even though I had a place to live, I'd still bounce from house to house. I thought this might make it tougher to keep track of me. I got mixed up with some pretty heavy characters. And things got crazier.

I wasn't a little guy any longer. Instead of making $200 deals, I'd make deals worth $1,000. That may not seem like a lot, but I wasn't one of those guys who made deals in the thousands of dollars. I was more of a street hustler.

Soon after graduation, I was doing $300 worth of cocaine a day. That's between three-and-a half to four grams at that time. Doing that much about five times a week would come to almost $80,000 a year. Just in coke. That total didn't include all the marijuana I smoked and all the alcohol I drank or all the pills I swallowed.

One night when I was eighteen, I overdosed on coke in the basement of a friend's house. I came out of my body and floated a few inches from the ceiling. I looked down and thought this is it. I sensed something behind me. A huge gold angel grabbed me, and in one of the sweetest, loving voices, said. "God is here with you, your life is not over yet. You have much more to live for than this

Jed." Then I immediately went back into my body. I opened my eyes. Mom stood over me in her place. I don't know how I got there.

I thought about quitting drugs a couple of times, usually when a friend died or I was so sick that I wanted to die. When someone you know straightens up, overdoses, gets sent to prison, or is murdered, that makes a person think about the lifestyle. But the pull, the adrenaline, is much too strong. It takes a lot more than a friend getting murdered for a person to give up drugs.

I did stop a handful of times, but only for a little while. Again, the pull was too strong. For someone who hasn't been addicted to drugs, the best comparison is the need to breathe. An addict often doesn't care about sleep or food. The addict lives only for the next bump, the next high.

Even getting arrested wasn't enough for me to give up the lifestyle. Of course, I thought about it. My first arrest was pretty stupid, and probably the craziest thing I ever did. I attended a party at the home of a wealthy friend. Her father worked for the Bureau of Criminal Apprehension. That night was crazy. So many people. So many drugs. People were everywhere throughout the house. Some were drinking. Others were doing drugs. People were having sex in just about every room.

I was all hopped on cocaine and went looking for alcohol. I knew her dad was a drinker. I searched the house and ended up in the master bedroom where I rifled through the dresser drawers. In one, I found a pistol. At the time I was a little down in the dumps. I grabbed the gun and everything that went with it. When I put the gun in my waistband, I thought that I shouldn't do this. But I did any way. I left, stole a car, and disappeared for two days.

The Bureau of Criminal Apprehension / Gang Strike Task Force found me at a friend's house. While on the run, I got high and became paranoid that everyone was out to get me. That was pretty intense. Being chased can be quite the high for a crook and drug dealer. I deemed that high greater than the drugs I sold or used. To me, it was all part of the game of the street life. But it also can be exhausting.

I crashed on a couch in the basement of a friend's house. While I slept, the authorities surrounded the house and brought in portable floodlights. At 4:00 a.m., I awoke to a strange noise and peeked out the window. In moments like this, a person doesn't think, instinct tells them to get out, run as fast as they can. I bolted out the back door. A group of armed men rushed me and dragged me down the steps.

I was thrown in the back of the cruiser and taken to the police station. A cop put me in a room, like they do criminals on television, and interrogated me until after daybreak about the whereabouts of the gun, bullets, and other stuff I stole. I didn't have the gun, though. I threw it in the St. Croix River in Stillwater, Minnesota.

I found out later that during their hunt for me, the cops knocked down twelve doors of homes that belonged to my family and friends. Two friends from Virginia were arrested because evidence relating to the gun and agent's badge was found in their vehicle. I didn't want them to get into trouble so I took the cops to the river to recover the gun.

After my arrest on felony charges for stealing the gun, I claimed mental instability. People knew I was trying to get off easy. And I was. I won't deny that. A doctor then diagnosed me with bi-polar. Most addicts know the symptoms and how to fake their actions. Unfortunately, this happens often.

I also knew I'd receive some type of rehabilitation or treatment. Looking back, I believe I was crying out for help before I really wanted it. I lied my way through the courts to get what I wanted, but at the same time I went through treatment, halfway giving the truth of what I really needed help for.

The second time I got busted for invading a home. I scoped out this other dealer who was known to keep a lot of cash and drugs at this place. Carrying only a knife, I broke in through the side door. I scoped out the place the night before, and assumed no one was home. I went through all five rooms, taking all valuables, a lot of money, bags of marijuana, as well as drug scales and paraphernalia. I decided to take a break in the house. I lit up a bong and smoked it until I was high. While chilling on a couch upstairs, I heard a noise coming from downstairs.

I went to investigate and discovered someone at the top of the stairs. I kicked them back down, ran from the house, hopped into my car, and sped off. I went to a friend's house where we'd been hanging out the past few weeks. The police kicked down the front door and found me hiding in a closet. I was shaking, my adrenaline through the roof.

I still had the knife on me, which could have been a first degree burglary charge. Instead, I was given a third degree charge because no one could prove my intent with the knife—to stab someone or use it to break in. Of course, I said I had it for the latter.

Thank goodness only the one guy came into the house. I honestly don't know what would have happened if a group of guys showed up. I may have cut one of them.

My third and fourth arrests were for possession of methamphetamines with intent to sell. Warrants were out for my arrest both times when I got picked up. One of the times the police found me at a hotel. I pushed the arresting officer when he tried to cuff me. I fought five cops at once until one of them used a Taser on me.

The other time I was bagging dope at home when cops entered. I bolted out the door. An officer stood on the porch and I kicked him into a snow bank. I thrived on that adrenaline. The cops needed just fifteen minutes or so to catch me. An officer shoved me in the back of the car. Most times I sat in silence or lashed out by punching things because I didn't want to go to jail. A person thinks a lot when they sit in the back of a police car. I usually thought about my mom or my brothers. This particular time, I cried for the first time in a long while. Another officer, one I knew from previous run-ins, asked if I thought I'd ever change. His question touched me, made me realize that someone really cared.

My story might sound glamorous to some, insane to others, and possibly unbelievable to a large majority. But I'm just one of thousands who have lived this lifestyle. Some were less involved, didn't sell as much or do as much dope as me. Others, like me, caved, and did a lot more. Much more than our body probably should have tolerated. It is truly only by the power and grace of God that I am still alive.

I lived one of those really sneaky and rebellious lives. You can see my story in a number of movies or television shows. You know, the one with the rebellious, lying, conniving, manipulating punk. The reality is that all this happened. And the effect it had on lives and the community is far beyond glamorous or worth idolizing on television or in movies. This lifestyle should be demonized on film, not made attractive. Filmmakers should expose this lifestyle for what it is, not for the money it can make. People need to see how hearts are hardened and families are ruined.

A lot of addicts are looking for a way to overcome. They want to hear about people who have victories. The more a person has overcome, the more powerful the story can be. But not everyone has to be an addict. We all have overcome something in our life. Some may feel they don't have a story because they haven't lived through the craziness that I did. These people don't understand they have a story too. They didn't cave like me.

They had a strength that kept them from doing anything stupid. They didn't give in even though the temptation was there.

I believe God kept me alive through all of this so He could later use my testimony to help millions who are trapped in darkness.

But my story of craziness was far from over.

Chapter 5

LOOKING OUT FOR ME

I soon discovered God was looking out for
me. Even when I was at my lowest, God sent people
into my life to get my attention. Some people don't
believe that's how God will operate, but I do. Some
feel that you need to make a trip to a holy land or
attend a big event, but that isn't always the case.
God reaches us right where we are. I was in no-go
places which made it difficult to find me. I moved
around because I was in search of someone to love
me, be real with me, tell me the truth, and help me
out of my mess.

God got my attention by sending people into

my path. Back then, I'd never have gone to a church service, revival, or any big event like that. People did invite me so I at least was aware of the events. Some may feel these were random acts, but I don't believe that. God sent those people to me. He does that. I've seen it happen multiple times. We'd be ready to get high or be right in the middle of doing something we shouldn't and someone would show up talking about God's love for us, and how He was calling us to a great life with Him.

I first noticed God was trying to get my attention in the mid-nineties. The first time this guy showed up at a park on school grounds across the street from my apartment complex, Birchwood Townhouse Apartments in Stillwater. My buddies and I smoked weed there when we could.

We noticed a guy wearing a cowboy hat walking down the hill toward us.

One of the guys said, "Put it out, put it out."

I'm like, "No, who cares." That's how I was back then.

When he got closer, we did put out our joints. He came right up to us. "What are you up to?"

He knew. The park was known as a place

where guys hung out to smoke or shoot up. I think he came by that day to evangelize. We chatted for a few minutes and then he asked if he could pray for us. We said he could, mostly just to get rid of him.

But God deposited something supernaturally in me that day. This guy was one example of someone going out of their way to offer help. That blew my mind. God gave him a word of knowledge and wisdom, and it stuck in me for a very long time.

Another time, in 1999, I'd been up three or four straight days using drugs. But I went to work anyway at a local office supply store in Stillwater. I was assigned to work the floor from my regular spot of shipping and receiving.

Early in my shift, three older people approached me in one of the aisles. The bearded man asked, "Could you help me find a pen please. Just one." I took him to appropriate aisle. He kneeled and pointed to the pen. "Can I have one of the pens from here? I don't want the whole package, I just need one pen."

"I cannot sell you just one pen," I said. "You need to buy the whole pack."

He stared at me, his gaze seeing something deep in me. "You are a very honest young man. What do you do for fun, outside of this work here?"

I couldn't believe he used that word—honest. That one little word pricked my life. I had a wad of cash in my pocket that I'd stolen from someone earlier that day. I thanked him and added, "I like to write and draw and kind of do whatever passes the time."

He introduced himself—Jacob Damkani from Tel-Aviv, Israel. We talked for forty minutes. My manager never bothered us, nor did any customers interrupted us. Jacob told me about his life and talked about Jesus.

Jacob prayed with me and gave me the book *Why Me?*—which I still have—before he left. Something changed in me, but not enough to quit my lifestyle for another five years during which God chipped away at my stony heart.

Jacob wandered into the store that day at the urging of the Holy Spirit. The way he reached me and the location where he reached me didn't matter. It mattered that God's heart was so for me that he sent someone completely out of the realm of anyone whom I would've listened to. He sent a surprise in the way of an interruption—from Israel to America—and it has impacted my life to this day.

Other times didn't work either, like the six times I spent in treatment centers from 1993-2004. Two were in jail, two in outpatient, which means I didn't live there, and two were long-term inpatient. My stays were court-ordered and usually pretty intense. The doctors and pastors did a lot of digging. They did everything they could—acupuncture, Chinese patches, yoga, music therapy, you name it, to get a person off the drugs and get the person healthy and sober.

At the first five treatment centers, I attended a number of drug rehabilitative meetings and sessions dealing with the addiction. We dealt with mostly surface issues, but never the roots, like life-controlling problems and issues. I also attended Alcoholics Anonymous and Narcotics Anonymous meetings. I didn't take those meetings serious so I didn't get much out of them, although I know they work for many.

I graduated from all the programs I went through. But, usually between two weeks and a month, I was back doing drugs, stealing stuff, and selling dope. The programs lacked any component that dealt with the sin issue I battled or helped me to see what God saw in me. I needed deliverance from a real devil who hated me, not a baby doll and pacifier bedded in lies and deception.

Most of my life I had my own agenda. I usually rehabbed to appease the courts. Going to these facilities either lightened my sentence or kept me out of jail altogether. I remember I attended a lot, and I mean a lot, of meetings. I said and did whatever I needed to get out. I was a pretty good liar. You need to be when you live a double life.

A lot of times when I went to court, I'd admit to everything. That was the best thing that ever happened. At the time I was genuine about the help. Unfortunately, the pull was greater than the commitment. People who have used understand this. No matter how much you want to change, and no matter how hard you try to change, that pull that need to get high, just eats away at you until you use again.

When a person hits the bubble, snorts a line, pops a pill, or smokes dope, they shift into what I call "Superman Mode." Nothing else matters. That person feels as if they have the power of the man with the blue cape. That is until the person crashes. Confusion. Lack of hope. That's how I felt when coming down. One of the worst feelings a person can experience.

That's sad too. A lot of people were pulling for me. People called me all the time to make sure I was okay. Every time I said yes, but the pain, the ache, grew each day. My mom cheered me on. I had all kinds of help. There was no reason that I couldn't do well. I just didn't want to give up the drugs or the lifestyle. I was so thick headed and hard-hearted. I didn't want to leave that lifestyle bad enough.

Looking back, if I had surrendered my life to the Lord earlier I wouldn't have had to go through what I went through. So much happened that you really can't comprehend what a person endures in that lifestyle. Every day is filled with danger. What was normal for us would freak out most law-abiding citizens. Crazy stuff. Overdosing. Getting caught in a crossfire.

During the summer of 2004 in East Saint Paul, Minnesota, at a time that I wanted to get out of the criminal activity, I almost got myself killed by being the middle man in the robbery of a drug dealer by another drug dealer. A friend and I were offered drugs and money to commit the robbery. I knew both dealers and didn't want to get involved. Instead, I took a small price to leave a door open for the place to get robbed.

Within forty-eight hours, the guys who got robbed found out my buddy and I were involved. They tracked us down and took us back to the house where they tortured us with guns and fed us drugs. They wanted me to overdose so it looked like they didn't kill me. One day, after being there for about two weeks, our captors led us to the basement. They shoved an AK-47 in my mouth and put a crossbow to my friend's face. I knew they were going to kill us. They had every reason to.

Then God intervened. My buddy's cell phone rang and he answered it. During the course of the quick conversation he mentioned where we were. I have no idea who called, but I'm convinced that if he hadn't mentioned our location, we would've been killed. Thinking they were now burned, the guys holding us ran out of the house.

I stood there with my buddy. My heart stopped somewhere between my chest and feet, not sure whether to race like a horse or stop. A power I didn't recognize at the time swept through the room. God supernaturally disarmed those guys right before my eyes. I believe someone was praying for us and He delivered us from death.

That was pretty scary. I messed up bad that time.

I still hadn't put myself in front of the one person I should—Jesus Christ. But that wasn't too far off. I would soon encounter the One who is greater than all.

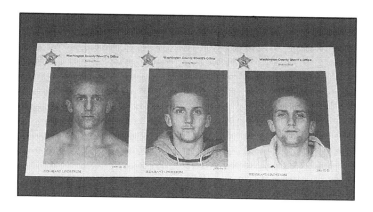

Jed's inmate photos from left to right: Washington County, Minnesota—1999, 2000, 2001. Jed was arrested and convicted on third-degree burglary, possession of stolen firearm, third-degree and fifth-degree controlled substance—use and distribution of methamphetamines / mushrooms / marijuana, pills, stolen items and scales.

From left: Jed's brother Hans, Jed, Jed's brother Chris.

Jed and Hans in Stillwater, Minnesota, on the St. Croix River.

Jed's brother Chris chilling in his car.

My beautiful mom Donna.

Reaching drug addicts in the streets, Jed ministers with his team under a bridge in Barranquilla, Colombia, in 2014.

Mobilizing and encouraging local churches in Barranquilla, Colombia. One of Jed's gifts include touching the hearts of God's people to reach the lost.

Ministry literature in English and Spanish going into the prisons, schools, streets and to families all over Colombia.

Freedom Experience, Lets Go Ministry's first Gospel Campaign, July 2014, in the Velodromo De Barranquilla, Colombia.

Holy Spirit power changes the lives of hundreds in Colombia.

Jed ministers to students at a Colombian school. After Jed spoke, the principal opened the school where Jed and his team spent hours praying for the sick and casting out devils.

Jed ministering with passion, exhorting the local churches to fall in love with Jesus all over again and to reach the lost.

Jed with Jacob Damkani, the man from Tel Aviv, Israel, who led Jed to Jesus in Stillwater, Minnesota. Jacob and Jed reunited and ministered together in Tel Aviv.

Tom Anderson, Jed's best friend from childhood. They are still close. Jed was able to lead Tom to the Lord and baptize him in the Chesapeake Bay in 2013.

Jed reunited with his daughter
Rosella after thirteen years
apart on July 30, 2014. They
spent their first day together at
Reunion Tower in Dallas.

Jed and his girls having fun!
Rosella, Annabelle and Lydia.

Jed and Erica married August
21, 2010. This pic was shot in a
studio in Manhattan a month
after their wedding.

Jed proposed to Erica in March
2010 at Split Rock Lighthouse
State Park, north of Duluth,
Minnesota.

Jed and his beautiful family near their home in Palm Coast, Florida, July 2015. From left: Jed, Annabelle, Erica, Lydia, and Rosella.

Learn more about Jed, his family and their ministry at www.letsgoministry.com. On their website you can place your personal prayer requests, get involved in the ministry, view more videos, pictures, track speaking engagements and mission adventures.

Chapter 6

UNDER THE INFLUENCE

People are quick to give drugs a chance, but not God. For reasons that I now don't understand, some would rather enjoy the physical stimulation of being spaced out more than the intimate feeling of being with the Lord. I've known both feelings quite well. I spent hours, days, even weeks strung out on drugs. I lost track of how many times I didn't know where I was.

Satan deceives every addicted person. He makes the person believe they never have enough. It's a trap. For me, it was an ever-increasing game, where there really is no satisfaction. So the thousands of dollars we made along with the increase of drugs we pushed may seem petty when compared to the crazy movies coming out of Hollywood.

I know thousands of families and young people were crushed and broken because of us. Communities feared us, but people there usually didn't take action until one of their kids got hooked.

I didn't like to sell cocaine and methamphetamine. I saw how these drugs destroyed families. But I also enjoyed the insane amount of money that rolled in and the lavish life of doing whatever I wanted to do, so I kept selling. When you're selling more, you're risking your life more. When you are risking your life to rob and steal, at some point you wonder if you've lost your mind.

No matter how much I wanted to get clean or quit the criminal activity, the pull was greater than the commitment. I buried so much pain back then that I'd do just about anything to keep it pushed far below the surface.

It's amazing that I am still alive. I put my body through so much. I could take a cat nap for fifteen minutes and that's all I needed. The average person sleeps eight to ten hours a day, goes to work, and is exhausted. You throw a group of criminals together who have stayed up all day, you can't imagine the stuff they get into or come up with. Parents with teenagers in that lifestyle really don't want to know. It's horrible the things that happen, to boys and girls alike. Stuff that I've seen.

Those in that lifestyle are there for a reason—they're searching, trying to fill a hole, heal a hurt, or hide something. That's why alcoholics drink. That's why people dive into porn. A large number turn to drugs.

That was me. I can't recall the number of times I got high, not even a guess. Even if I did know, I'm not sure knowing would've made a difference. All I wanted to do was fill that hole in my life.

People think they know what, or who, has caused the hole. They don't, until the hole is filled with the right thing. Or person. I thought my hole was not having my dad in my life. He wasn't. I discovered that person was Jesus Christ.

But I still had some stuff to go through, stuff that I look back on and realized that if I paid attention to His trying to get my attention, I wouldn't have suffered through some of the crap that I put me, my family, and God through. Yes, God. I learned that when we don't obey Him, we hurt Him, just like we hurt or wound an earthly parent. Because He loves us deeper than any human could, His pain is much, much deeper. And we don't even know it. Worse, we might not care and end up hurting ourselves.

Instead of God, I leaned heavily on quick fixes—drugs and other people. Like nearly everyone in that environment, I didn't take responsibility for my actions. Not until a person has that awakening, either through the guiding power of the Holy Spirit or a court order that opens their eyes, does a person begin to take responsibility. Even then, it can take a while to take hold.

Some doctors, on the other hand, want to solve issues with medication, like they did with me. That's not the solution. Medication doesn't get to the root of the problem. Medication places a bandage on the problem. Now, I do believe at certain times a person does need the support of medication. But I feel it should be done with the very, very minimum. I don't think multiple medications at once should be the answer. Throwing a ton of medication at a problem pushes God aside. I believe medication was never meant to be a permanent solution. Jesus is our healer.

I know there is another way and I believe that is part of my message—a message of freedom, liberating people from their own bondage. We cannot break free in our own strength. We need

God's power to escape, not only from our own bondage of things like porn, drugs, criminal activity, but also from demonic strongholds.

The word of God is healing to our bodies. When we stand on His word, we receive health. I was healed overnight from Zoloft and Neurontin that I was court ordered to take. I was in jail and was told that "we can't make you take it, but if you don't, you'll be in violation of your probation. You do what you gotta do."

I wouldn't take it anymore. It was messing me up, and I haven't taken it since 2001.

My work now is to help people break out from the influence of the enemy and live victoriously with God. That's why I repeatedly contact anyone who may be struggling. It could be a teenager whose parents are concerned. It could be the parents of a wayward teenager, I know from God's work in my life and with those I've ministered to, He wants families restored and healed.

Some are trapped in that lifestyle. They feel they'll die in there. They know that and don't care. They live without hope.

That lifestyle can be lonely. The waiting times are the worst. You wait days for your next fix.

Those are the days when really bad things happen. You make bad decisions. You face a lot of rejection and abandonment. You worry that your family has given up on you.

I've had friends kick me out of their car because they got word the cops were looking for me. I'd roam the streets for days. I couldn't go home. I couldn't go to a friend's house. One time a family found me sleeping along the road and put me on their front porch. When I woke up, they asked me to leave.

I slept on park benches. I dug through clothing bins of a well-known contribution center. I remember some nights just scrapping together enough money to buy a donut and a coffee. Often I didn't smell good. Sometimes I'd go a week between showers.

At times, I was so tired and strung out that I wanted to give up on life. I almost committed suicide a few times. I believe divine protection kept me alive through what seemed innocent contact with others. Someone who came along at the right time with a word of knowledge or wisdom probably happened more than I knew. Other times someone might have made a comment that it appeared I was having a bad day. We'd share a quick laugh and they'd move on. Or other times I might tell them they have no idea and their look of compassion gave me hope.

The power of God is so underestimated. In those moments, like when someone who didn't know me took me in and fed me, we don't understand what God is doing. Only later are we able to look back and see His work.

Down on my luck, lonely, smelling bad, I often wondered if anyone would love me. I'd walk by homes and see kids playing with a parent, especially a dad, and yearn for a "real" life. Or I was the person on the sidewalk with a puppy dog face or yelling at the air that families saw from the comfort of their living room. Yes, I was that guy sometimes.

A mess.

In my story, people can see how difficult my life was. I can't deny that. In the midst, though, I still cared about the people. I looked out for them. Not just those in my group, but the people I robbed, manipulated, and stole from.

The Shepherd again went after the one stray. He never gave up on me.

Even during the time when I thought about killing someone. I was at the end of my rope and hanging out with this kid about fifteen years old. We got messed up one night. I wanted his car and his cash. So I took us for a little ride to the edge of town. The kid didn't have a clue I planned to kill him. He sat in the passenger seat, laughing and cutting up with me. During the drive, the whole thing shifted. I think God changed my heart.

I wish I would have heeded the warnings earlier. I believe if someone—a doctor, a friend, a family member—would have leaned on me harder, I might not have gone down this path. I'm not blaming them for what I did. They didn't give up on me.

Their persistence paid off at the Law Enforcement Center Correction in St. Paul, Minnesota, on October 11, 2004. I was on the run from the police, but my mom found me and drove me to the center. During the drive, she cried and prayed out loud for the Lord to change me. Just hours after my mom dropped me off, I knelt on that cold jail cell floor and begged God to spare my life. I surrendered my life to Jesus, was filled with the Holy Spirit and began to speak in tongues praying and praising God.

My life since has become a testimony to what God can do.

Chapter 7

A NEW PERSON IN CHRIST

Before I begged God to change me, I thought I'd die soon. I weighed 100 pounds, about seventy pounds less than I do now. I walked into the jail house wearing dirty jeans and a T-shirt. I may have and may not have taken a shower in the last couple of days. That wasn't important.

I was suicidal and homicidal. I didn't really want to kill myself, but the thought came to mind. After being booked, I was put in a cell where an officer asked how I felt. I said, "I don't have anything to live for." He said he'd pretend that he didn't hear that. Otherwise, procedure called for him to put me in a straight-jacket and on suicide watch.

Because of my priors, I faced a mandatory thirty-three months in prison. I sat on the edge of the thin mattress and let random thoughts tumble through my mind. I didn't focus on any particular thing. I spaced out. Once in a while, I remembered the words my mother spoke during the thirty-minute drive to the jail, "You're my son. I want you to live."

My mom and I endured a long-lasting relationship of fighting and verbally assaulting each other. I started most of the fights, but she never gave up on me. I think I gave up because she never did. I know she never stopped praying. The Holy Spirit stopped me from going on the run. He sent my mom to help me, His way of intervening again.

I lived moment to moment in the cell. I didn't have any plans. With no clear thought, no agenda, no reason, I simply slid onto the floor and sat on my knees Crying, I sat for a long time, until I shivered from the cold of the floor. At first, I didn't say or think much. Eventually, I mumbled, "God fill me up." I repeated that over and over. Then I said, "Change me. I don't want to live like this."

I knew if I didn't change, I'd die this way.

My words became more desperate. I sensed something stirring deep inside me. A yearning to really change, as well as a concept foreign to me—to be changed. A strong desire to live replaced my thoughts of hurting myself or others.

I grabbed a Bible someone had left in the cell. After years of people telling me about God, I sought him earnestly for the first time. I remember reading a passage, Ephesians 4:28, that said, "thieves steal no longer." I wondered if that meant ever again. I really had no clue of what honest living was all about.

In my cell, I experienced the real feeling of a person wrapping their arms around me. I knew it was God, even with my limited knowledge of faith. He held me for a long time. I relaxed in the peace that seeped into my being. The more I relaxed the more He removed the pain, the hatred that drove me for more than ten years. He replaced those feelings with His love.

I prayed for Him to fill me with the Holy Spirit and I began praying in the Holy Spirit soon after. His Word came alive to me. I didn't know which scriptures to read. Most times I flipped open the Bible and read random passages. Most say this isn't the way to read the Bible, but God divinely took me to the words He wanted me to read. I spent a lot of time in the Word. I felt a change in my heart.

People noticed my change right away. The hardness of my "anything that goes life" dissipated. I physically felt the difference, like God unraveled me so He could put me back together.

Every day, something broke inside me. I felt more guilt about all the ungodly things I did. The lies. The anger. The deceit. The manipulation. One could say I was a piece of work back then.

I don't think people realize how tied up they are until they've been loosened by the power of God. Many people's emotional issues affect their body with tense shoulders, backs, or stomachs. When the Holy Spirit touches those areas, He brings freedom and the person can move freely. That's what I feel happened to me. And I've seen it with many others.

I let go of things I didn't know I held onto— insecurities, pain, guilt, forgiveness, anguish, desperation. Some people have described this feeling as a physical weight leaving their body, like a heavy rock falling off their shoulder. For me, the experience was more of an emotional breaking, followed by healing. I love that about God. He liberates those that the enemy has bound.

I thought of my friend Tommy. As kids, we called each other daily, biked to school, and threw a baseball around for fun. On weekends we stayed up all night, laughing and playing. Unsure why he popped into my mind, I wrote and told him everything. To my surprise, he wrote back. He forgave me. Better than that, he wrote that he believed that I needed this change. This confirmed what I'd felt. My change was real and not a figment of my imagination. I needed others to help, love, and forgive me for my wrongs to them. And they did. I discovered that if I forgive, I will also be forgiven. In 2013, I led Tommy to Jesus and shortly after baptized my childhood friend in the Chesapeake Bay in Norfolk, Virginia.

Some of my old buddies from the outside ended up in my POD, where the jail kept forty to eighty of us. Most of them got word about the change in me and wanted to see if it was real. When we hung out, I talked about God's work in my life. I didn't judge them, but I did have an impact. I could see that. I hoped they would believe the change in me and accept that God loved them too. I wanted them to experience what was happening to me, the incredible change taking place. I knew God used me to speak into their lives. A lot of times, though, people don't want to hear the word from someone who used to run with them. It wasn't my place to change them, just plant a seed, like many had done in my life.

I didn't give my life to Jesus because I was in a jail cell. I truly surrendered my whole life to the lordship and love of Jesus. Some of my old buddies might not have been sure my change would stick. That's understandable. Sometimes, it doesn't.

God moved fast in me.

By the time I appeared before the judge for my sentencing, I looked and felt different. A peace surrounded me that I barely understood. Despite the change in me, I was a little nervous the judge would hold to the mandatory sentence. He didn't.

Hardened criminals, people without remorse, spaced out individuals stand before judges every day in court rooms around the country. I think the judge saw a broken man in me. I'd been radically changed by the power of the Holy Spirit. Jesus was all over my life. When I stood before the judge, he said something that shocked me. "I don't know why, but I will have mercy." I knew why. God intervened. "If you are interested, I will send you to back to Minnesota Adult and Teen Challenge."

I'd already been through Minnesota Adult and Teen Challenge before, so at age twenty-four

I'd face some of people who already had shown me love and grace.

Shocked, I didn't respond for a minute. Radical. Mercy. God. Those words slammed into my mind. I couldn't resist God's plan for me. I took the judge's offer.

In early November 2004 I entered the restoration program for graduates. This program is customized for each patient based on needs. I needed seven months. Some stay shorter, some longer. In the program, I experienced the same love I felt in my jail cell, love that helped me understand someone wanted me to succeed in life. Joy replaced guilt. Hope replaced fear. God brushed off the dirt, and again I had a reason to live.

I woke up every morning and prayed. I became more motivated each day, which rubbed off on others around me. In the morning, I learned about worship and prayer, listened to guest speakers, and attended classes for personal study for new Christians. In the afternoon, I spent a lot of time cleaning, a humbling experience for someone who ignored these menial tasks for the previous eleven years. I scrubbed toilets, wiped down kitchen counters, washed clothes. After I'd been there a while, I helped people move. I remember standing in one guy's house, holding something, and thinking a year ago I'd stolen this.

I learned how to live a criminal-free life. This new life felt "right." I saw what it was like to honestly work. I knew how to work, but now I worked for someone else—the Lord.

I grew a lot in Minnesota Adult and Teen Challenge. I dreamed again with vision and the will to be a man of integrity honoring God with my life. I wanted to live a full life. From 1993-2004, I thought I did. And I understand why a person in a criminal lifestyle might feel they are. But until they experience the move of the Holy Spirit in their life, they have no idea how pitiful the old ways really are.

Near the end of my stay in Minnesota Adult and Teen Challenge, I enrolled in the recently started Bible school. I felt called into the ministry of reconciliation and needed more help understanding God's word, what He was calling me into, and equipping me for the work ahead. I wanted to help others out of bondage and into freedom, a new life only God can reveal to a broken soul.

My life since has become a testimony to what He can do when one brings their broken life to a living God who loves, heals, and cares deeply for them.

Chapter 8

NEW BEGINNING, NEW ADVENTURES

For the next three years I lived in various places in my home state of Minnesota. I graduated in 2007 from the Minnesota Adult and Teen Challenge Bible School, now called the Leadership Institute, with an associate degree in biblical studies and Christian leadership.

I went back to the streets after that. Not to slip into my old ways. This time to spread the Word of God. Backed by Ripe for Harvest World Outreach, based in Mesa, Arizona, I operated as a U.S. missionary in street evangelism. Walking the streets with God as my guide was so much better than when I spent days upon days on the street. I also ministered to inmates when the opportunities arose.

After graduating from the Leadership Institute, I lived on $250 a month and slept on an air mattress in a house I shared with two other friends in Northeast Minneapolis. Everything I owned fit into a two small suitcases. I stacked my clothes near the mattress. The suitcases served as my dresser.

Doesn't sound glamorous. Full of God's joy, I was content. I trusted Him with my provisions. When we give our life to the Lord, we usually don't inherit mounds of cash or are given a new BMW or even guaranteed perfect health. God provides, lavishly sometimes. He doesn't always give us what we think we need. He blesses us as we have need. What we get in Christ is His will for our life, our healing, and our provisions. In many cases, that means giving up a lot of the material things we treasured.

Almost every day I traveled by bus to downtown Minneapolis to minister with others in the streets. We shared the love of Jesus with powerful testimonies that followed as God confirmed His word with power and a demonstration of His love. Daily we saw lives impacted, people healed, and others set free from whatever demonic strongholds that bound them.

One time outside a steakhouse in Minneapolis, through the Holy Spirit, I told a doctor that God knew how to heal him. His eyes widened. He'd not told me about any illness or disease. God made this doctor aware that He knows a person's greatest need. We prayed and the doctor commented on the shift he felt in his heart. I smiled, knowing it was a physical healing.

I remember another young man walking in a group down the street toward me. The Holy Spirit showed me a vision of a knife and this kid. I greeted him when he walked past. He glared at me and kept walking. I yelled at his back, "You don't want to give up today. God is waiting for you to put in His hand where it hurts you the most."

He stopped and turned to me. With his friends listening, he said that he cut himself to drive away his pain. When finished, he gave me the knife and he let me pray with him for eternal life.

In 2009, I sat on the Long Beach sand in New York City and prayed. God said, "Ask me anything in my name and I will give it to you." At first, I couldn't think of anything until the yearning for a wife surfaced. Not more than a year later, He moved in my life in a huge way. I started dating a woman named Erica.

We'd known each other for some time. Whenever I traveled through Duluth, Minnesota, her family, the Saylers, always loved me and opened their doors. Her family showed me the love of God in so many ways. Until then, I never knew what a healthy family looked like.

Erica and I sensed God wanted us together. We started dating in February 2010. A month later, I proposed to her on Split Rock just north of Duluth along the north shore of Lake Superior. We married less than six months later in West Duluth. Four months after that, in obedience to God's saying, "grow roots and branch out," Erica and I moved to Daytona Beach, Florida. Through agreement in prayer, we believed the Lord wanted us to start a family here, and a ministry called Lets Go Ministry.

Erica, who previously worked a short time as children's pastor at a small church in Florida, and I left family in Minnesota. Although it hurt to leave them behind, we knew God had our family in His care. The tears of sorrow soon turned to joy.

Before the New Year, we launched the ministry which had been stirring in me since 2006. The call felt so rich in my heart that I couldn't do anything else. Some people would call this "being consumed by the Holy Spirit" or "led into a divine call". I just knew it was a divine call upon my life.

My desire to spread His word grew with this mandate. Nothing else mattered.

With His guiding hand, Lets Go Ministry has grown into a Kingdom fire on earth. We share His love with everyone we possibly can. At the writing of this book, we've currently ministered in twenty-six states and five countries.

He has opened numerous doors for the ministry, starting with one that allowed me to travel freely around the world. When I first traveled from Minnesota to New York City on short-term mission trips, I needed the permission in writing from my probation officer to leave. I checked in when I returned. My probation was scheduled to last twenty years until 2021. In 2012, God released me from the probation nine years early.

Since 2006 I've visited New York City more than twenty times. The first trip came in July of that year. I arrived in the Big Apple with my friend David and 300 Bibles. I gave the first one to a man named Luis. He'd never owned a Bible, nor heard about Jesus. I knew that through this encounter God was doing a deep work in me as well as those I ministered to. David and I walked the streets of the city that never sleeps thinking New York needed a heavy dose of the God who never sleeps.

I spent the first four years of my ministry

traveling back and forth to New York, as well as to a handful of other cities in the U.S. I shared about God in the streets and subways, in the sun and rain, in the spring and fall. While there during one trip, God birthed in me a heart for the nations. After my probation ended, God opened the door for international ministry.

With more than enough to do locally, I didn't want to venture into international ministry. Our primary areas of ministry have been the Daytona Beach and Orlando areas, as well as New York City, the Twin Cities, and northern Minnesota.

God has sent me to Colombia, Puerto Rico, Germany, Africa, and Israel where I was able to minister alongside evangelist Jacob Damkani, the man who led me to Jesus. Now, after numerous trips out of the country, I have a bigger heart for the nations.

I've been to Barranquilla, Colombia, five times. We've reached thousands and launched our first-ever "Freedom Experience Gospel" campaign in the infamous Velodromo De Barranquilla, a small professional bicyclist stadium.

Over the years we have seen thousands come to know the saving, healing, and delivering power of Jesus there in the Department of Atlántico. In one of the most powerful moves of the Holy

Spirit, I witnessed a crammed house full of people in Carrizal give their lives to the Lord.

After a long morning of ministering, I headed back to base to rest. Before I could lie down, a young boy came to the door with Pastor Romo. He explained this young boy came with a message for the missionaries. His grandmother witnessed her son's murder—just fifteen feet from her—a few days before. She wanted us to come pray with her.

I left with the boy and Pastor Romo. While we walked, it seemed in the supernatural everything was shaking still. We arrived to find the entire family crammed into a small house. No air conditioning. Sweating from head to toe. The mother sat in her chair, weeping. The family stood in silence.

I prayed and asked the Holy Spirit to come and comfort this family. He did, and we spent an hour with them. More people arrived. Soon we couldn't move. We prayed again. Every single person in the house surrendered to Jesus. To this day, they serve in the local church.

Through the years, God has opened the door for me to share His love with many of my old friends. I've been privileged to lead them to the One who knows them the most. I think many times, "who am I to speak into their life, I mean I was not long ago doing the very same thing they are doing."

Having witnessed countless experiences, I know Jesus is alive. He does miracle after miracle. And He still had one planned for me.

Chapter 9

RESTORATION

I walked to the mailbox one day after returning home from a grueling trip to Barranquilla, Colombia. An envelope with the return address of the department of family and protective services sat on top. Nervous, I hurried into the house to open it in front of my wife Erica. I began to read, and my heart raced like a junkie in need of a fix.

Erica touched my arm. "What is it, Sweetie"?

"I think this is my daughter and they want to get in touch with me about something that has happened to her."

Rosella—a girl I fathered during a six month on-again, off-again relationship. Erica knew that I might have a daughter. I never tried to keep it from her. When Rosella was born, my name wasn't included on her birth certificate. I stayed with the birth mom for a few months. But my condition didn't permit me to offer much in the way of parenting. I soon left Rosella's mother and we agreed it was best to keep her in the care of her grandparents. I always questioned if I did the right thing.

I read the letter with memories of this little girl flitting through my mind. The Holy Spirit saturated me with grace and peace. I knew my past failures would not dictate my future and God would turn it around for good. More importantly, this young girl needed my help. Who knows what happened to her or what she was going through? Right now she needed a dad to step up and care for her. I knew immediately I needed to take responsibility, and seek out if Rosella was really my daughter.

After reading the letter, Erica and I called the number enclosed. "Is she okay?" Erica asked, showing compassion for a person she didn't know. She wanted to know why I didn't try harder to find this girl. I asked myself that same question countless times. But I lost touch with the grandparents and mother. I convinced myself that not knowing meant she must be in a safe place. Rosella wasn't.

I spoke with Rosella's case worker. She informed us Rosella had been placed in foster care after being abused. The pain in my heart—like an ice pick through the middle—was not imagined. Through tears, I looked at Erica. Tears rolled down her cheeks. When I hung up and without saying a word, I knew Erica and I would care for this girl. The case worker asked me to get tested through a court order. Erica and I agreed that even if I wasn't the biological father, God would have us care for this young girl. In my heart, though, I already knew the result—Rosella was my daughter. More importantly, we'd go to any lengths to get her.

For the next few days, I couldn't stop thinking about Rosella. The story of her abuse and the reality of what she may be feeling sunk in deep to my spirit. I couldn't shake it off. It hung on me like a wet poncho. I could only begin to see what God was doing here and I knew I needed to be patient, yet ready to take action at any minute.

Erica and I cried and prayed. Together we received confirmation we would rescue Rosella. Knowing my limitations, I knew this was a stirring from my heavenly Father. He placed all the right people in my life to make this happen. No one could deny God's hand in this. Yet, the thought lingered, "how would God work this miracle?"

After years of ministering to boys and girls—many runaways without families—around the world and seeing the miracles God does in them was He working one for me? I know every precious life is immeasurably valuable. The addict in a mansion and the broken soul under a bridge are comparable in the eyes of God. He has no favorites. God loves us all too much for us to be thrown away by any other person. What man throws away God raises up to a living testimony of His power and love.

As a man of God, I'd traveled to numerous places and shared God's love to others. I quickly discovered my own brokenness and lack of love I simply needed more of the Holy Spirit to fill me again. I was in desperate need of God's grace to touch me and help me to see what He was seeing and trying to reveal to me. Yes, I left behind a little girl when I should have done more. God knew this was the time to bring Rosella and I back together. In fact, the perfect time. At no other time in my life could I have taken in Rosella. I couldn't have cared for her up until now. He knew that. And now was giving me a second chance with my daughter whom I thought I'd never see again.

Erica said God placed something on her heart weeks before getting this letter that she would care for a young girl, someone who was in need of help. In my heart, this felt like a mission from heaven—everything that we love to do in our ministry and as a family. Rosella became our greatest mission to date. The DNA test confirmed Rosella was my daughter. What joy, what relief, what pain from years past—wasted years that God was restoring and healing now.

I went to Texas to reunite with Rosella. For her, to meet me. An infant when I left, she kept a photo of me in case she ever did meet her daddy. We spent our first day together—on my thirty-fourth birthday—at the top of the Reunion Tower in downtown Dallas. Later that night we enjoyed a baseball game together.

During the first court appearance God opened the door for a two-week visit. I didn't expect that. She cried—tears of joy in knowing she could get to know her father and his family, and tears of sorrow for her siblings left behind in Texas. Only the sun shone brighter than her smile on that trip.

We received full custody of Rosella in April 2015.

After walking through fire—praying and

wondering about the "what ifs"—did I realize that I was in the middle of a great miracle. God reconciled my daughter to me. Every day with her has become a celebration of God's redeeming glory. I guess sometimes a person must go through the fire to experience great miracles.

I reunited with my daughter during Lets Go Ministry's Freedom Experience where God brought families together. The mission was to see households saved, and to see the hearts of the fathers turned to their sons, and the fatherless brought back into relationship with their family. This very reality unfolded in my life as fruit of the Holy Spirit at work.

God started this work in me long before Rosella came to us. He prepared my whole family. He does that, He prepares us to receive His best and we have to walk with God no matter how the day looks, knowing we can trust God. The Lord knew I needed a deep work in my heart before He would use me to reach others at this capacity.

God did a deep work in my heart so I could persevere with love and grace to others who are need. Even today, multitudes live without family and without loved ones to care for and protect them from this evil world. Because of another great work by my Lord, Rosella is not among those.

Thirteen years before I didn't know what to do with my life. So I had no idea what to do with another's life in my care. Now I do know, now that I know the heart of God is for souls, for people to really know God, not just hear about Him. People look for people who demonstrate God's love. God desires that all would know His great love.

What I thought was my greatest mistake— leaving this baby girl behind—turned out to be a testimony to God's redeeming power. A true blessing of reconciliation. Only the Lord could do something so personal, so special. He will take care of the rest of the details that we cannot understand.

He restores. He gives second chances. He returns what should be brought back. Like my little girl.

Chapter 10

RECONCILIATION

If I have learned one thing in walking with the Lord, it is this: He loves to save people from hell and death. He loves to reveal His power and never-ending love. He loves to heal the sick and the broken. He loves to see the lame walk. He loves to snatch us from the hands of the enemy. He loves it when we pray, seek His face.

I know, and after reading my story you know, that's what He did with me. Satan ran rampant in my life until I turned from Satan and to the Lord. That's when God revealed Himself to me.

I am a living testimony of God's power.

Doesn't matter the amount of drugs I took or the heinous crimes I committed, there was never a moment in my life that God didn't love me. More than ten years after falling to my knees in my jail cell, I still live out of the goodness of God. I watch Him work miracles every day. I'm not ashamed to share what He has done in me. He still saves today. He still heals today. He still loves you today, no matter what you have done.

God restores.

Only the Lord could do something so personal, so special. I can sing and I can shout praises to Him because of His plan of redemption.

We may think we have it all together, that we have all the answers, or that we know what is best for us. We don't. His plan is always higher than ours. Always. Through prayer and extended time in His presence, I can hear His voice and know His plans as He reveals them to me step by step. He speaks clearly and He moves in great power. There is nothing too hard for God. When He makes a promise, He keeps it. You can trust Him.

If someone knew everything about you and still loved you beyond anything you've felt before, how close would you want to get to this person? If this person provided a way to remove all the guilt of your past and all of the stains of your mistakes, would you want it?

If you've wavered on your answer, consider this:

Can I move forward in my life today living the way I am living?

Probably not. You may need help from the One who loves you the most.

Today is your day of salvation! Today is your day of healing and deliverance! Will you fully surrender your life to Jesus today?

HELPFUL SCRIPTURES

John 3:16-18

"For this is how God loved the world: He gave his one and only Son, so that everyone who believes in him will not perish but have eternal life. God sent his Son into the world not to judge the world, but to save the world through him. "There is no judgment against anyone who believes in him. But anyone who does not believe in him has already been judged for not believing in God's one and only Son.

Romans 3:23

For everyone has sinned; we all fall short of God's glorious standard.

Matthew 3:2

"Repent of your sins and turn to God, for the Kingdom of Heaven is near."

Acts 3:17-20

"Friends, I realize that what you and your leaders did to Jesus was done in ignorance. But God was fulfilling what all the prophets had foretold about the Messiah—that he must suffer these things.

Now repent of your sins and turn to God, so that your sins may be wiped away. Then times of refreshment will come from the presence of the Lord, and he will again send you Jesus, your appointed Messiah.

John 10:10

The thief's purpose is to steal and kill and destroy. My purpose is to give them a rich and satisfying life.

2 Corinthians 5:18

"and all of this is a gift from God, who brought us back to himself through Christ. And God has given us this task of reconciling people to him."

Malachi 4:6

"His preaching will turn the hearts of fathers to their children, and the hearts of children to their fathers. Otherwise I will come and strike the land with a curse."

Psalm 68:4-6

"Sing praises to God and to His name! Sing loud praises to His who rides on the clouds. His name id the Lord – rejoice in His presence! Father to the Fatherless, defender of widows –this is God, whose dwelling is holy."

Romans 12:1

"and so dear brothers and sisters, I plead with you to give your bodies to God because of all He has done for you. Let them be a living and holy sacrifice – the kind He will find acceptable."

Matthew 6:10

May your Kingdom come soon.
May your will be done on earth,
as it is in heaven.

Matthew 6:33-34

Seek the Kingdom of God above all else, and live righteously, and he will give you everything you need. "So don't worry about tomorrow, for tomorrow will bring its own worries. Today's trouble is enough for today.

Ephesians 1:5

God decided in advance to adopt us into his own family by bringing us to himself through Jesus Christ. This is what he wanted to do, and it gave him great pleasure.

RESPOND TO GOD'S CALL

God has been good to me. In this book, I only scratched the surface of His marvelous blessings during my walk with Him. I thought I'd die a lying, thieving, worthless drug addicted criminal. I told God many times that I was sorry. I never meant it until October 11, 2004.

I remember God saying, "Jed, I forgive you. I cleanse you by the blood of my Son."

He will say the same thing to you when you repent of your sins and fully surrender to Him. Go to Him as you are. You don't need to get cleaned up to go to church. Go to church and get cleaned up. Watch Him work a miracle in your life.

I encourage you to not wait another day. I encourage you to live for Him—with no reservations. Yes, have godly boundaries but live courageously for Him. You will be part of His plan for this time, and declare His wonderful handiwork.

I wrote this book because I believed God has called you into deeper intimacy with Him. He wants you to tell people about what led you to repentance. When you fully surrender your life to Jesus, you will know. He will reveal Himself to you. I suggest you write the date and time somewhere in this book so you can share that experience with others.

A simple plan for a healthy balance in life has helped me in my walk with the Lord. Either use these quick steps to begin your walk or use them to strengthen your walk. For more information about each can be found on our website, www.letsgoministry.com.

SEVEN BASIC STEPS TO FOLLOW JESUS

1. Examine your life
What you received, eternal life is powerful, and He will radically change your heart and life from this point on. As you open your heart though the Holy Spirit, examine yourself, you will fall deeper in love with God and know His heart more clearly.

2. Surround yourself with healthy support
You need others around you who can speak into your life. Submit yourself to a local life-giving, Holy Spirit-filled church. When you find one, introduce yourself to the pastor or leader, share with them how you have fully surrendered your life to

Jesus, and you want to know how to grow in your relationship with God. Don't go to church and hide.

3. Take care of your body

You may have some life-controlling habits, possibly drug addiction, pornography, wrong eating patterns, laziness. Whatever it may be, that habit affects your body at some level. Look at your habits and ask God if He wants you to change them. Don't fight His answer. The more time you spend with Him, the clearer you will hear Him. This is really a call to personally holiness, intimacy with God and right living. Consider exercise as well, and get help from people who know about this, not people who talk about it.

4. Accountability and discipleship

Find one or two mature believers who can walk with you as a mentor and hold you accountable as you grow in God. Someone willing to walk with you through the ups and downs of life. As you grow with the Lord, ask Him to send you someone you can be a mentor to, and disciple them in the word of God and encourage them in their new walk with Jesus.

5. Personal prayer life

Prayer is a responsibility and honor. Seek God in every situation and opportunity so you can know

His will clearly. Your personal prayer life also will lead you to times of fasting and corporate prayer—with others for families, communities, cities, and nations. Don't be afraid to pour out your heart to God in your language, with your words. Make a list if one will help.

6. Be baptized in water and the Holy Spirit

You need the power of God in every circumstance. Being baptized in water is a public declaration of your allegiance to Him. You also need the power of the Holy Spirit. When baptized in the Holy Spirit, you will pray in the Holy Spirit, new tongues will be uttered as you pray and God will reveal—to you or through another person—through interpretation what that means while you pray.

7. Go with confidence and in love with God

Share your great news with others. With as many people as you can. Tell them about what Jesus has done, and is doing, in your life. Don't be shy. In the streets, in the jails, in the marketplaces wherever God sends you, go, in the power of the Holy Spirit and in the love of God and let Him use you for His glory. Let Jesus manifest His life through yours and radically change the environment wherever you go. You cannot turn this life with Jesus on and off as you desire. Always burn hot for Jesus.

I am a personal witness to the miraculous works of Jesus Christ. By the power of the Holy Spirit bodies are made whole, the demon possessed are set free and placed in their right mind, the lost are saved and brought eternal life and hope and the lame walk and the deaf hear.

In the Bible we read about God's desire for His kingdom to touch the earth so He can changes whatever or whomever He touches. That could be you. That should be you. I believe God will use this book to inspire you to live for Jesus and follow Jesus all the days of your life.

God did a great work in me. The same kind of great work He can do in you, when you are ready to break out.

ORDER MORE BOOKS

Order more books today for your ministry, organization, or to give to others.

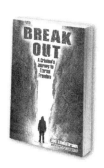

<u>**Donate Books:**</u> You can purchase a bulk of books for Let's Go Ministry to freely give to others who are in need of hearing a story of hope and restoration. This is not tax deductible, but allows the ministry to help others!

<u>**Bulk Order Discounts:**</u> Shipments are available of 50+ books at a time. If you are interested in buying bulk, contact us at www.jedsbook.com.

<u>**Give as a Gift:**</u> Break Out makes a great gift for others in your life.

<u>**Purchase Books to Sell at Your Store:**</u> The book is available for you to sell at your church or store.

<u>**Small Group Study:**</u> You may also order books as part of a small group or Bible study.

Find out more at www.jedsbook.com

ABOUT LETS GO MINISTRY

Evangelist Jed Lindstrom is the founder and director of Lets Go Ministry (LGM), an independent evangelistic ministry that seeks to bring transformation to individuals and communities through the power of the Gospel.

Jed is a 2005 graduate of Minnesota Adult & Teen Challenge and a 2007 graduate of the Teen Challenge Leadership Institute (TCLI). He is best known for his creativity and boldness while ministering the Gospel in some of the darkest places in the United States. The vision of LGM to take the Gospel to the "No Go Places" was given to Jed in 2006 while in TCLI. Since that time, Jed has ministered in over 50 cities in 26 states and in 5 countries, impacting over 10,000 souls with the Gospel message.

LGM is based in Daytona Beach, Florida, where Jed lives with his wife, Erica, and three daughters, Rosella, Annabelle and Lydia.

Find out more at www.letsgoministry.com

INVITE JED TO SPEAK

Do you have a special event coming up? Would you like to someone to come for exhortation or evangelism purposes? Jed Lindstrom is available to speak at your event, including:

- Prison Ministry
- Engagements at church
- Special events
- Bible Schools/Colleges, Treatment Centers and Discipleship Programs
- Public schools with a full opportunity to share the gospel
- Or give us your idea!

To schedule Jed, contact Lets Go Ministry on the web at: www.letsgoministry.com or www.jedsbook.com

FROM THE DESK OF RUSSELL HOLLOWAY

I first traveled with Jed Lindstrom to New York City in July 2011. We encouraged hard-working pastors who labored around the city. We fed the homeless. We prayed with dozens of people outside a Starbucks in the Wall Street area of Lower Manhattan. Many times I witnessed the power of Jed's personal testimony.

His life story isn't just for the lost, or the poor, or the addict. His story resonates with anyone who is open to Jesus' message of love and redemption.

I ask that you support Jed and Lets Go Ministry. My wife and I want to provide free books to as many people as possible. Please prayerfully consider joining us in supporting Jed's efforts to go into the "no-go" places with the saving message of Jesus.

God has been and will be glorified for years to come by Jed's story and message. Let's all work together to lift up the name of Jesus.

Russell Holloway, MS, LMHC, NCC
Director of Counseling Services, Port Orange Counseling Center, Ormond Beach Counseling Center, and Daytona Beach Marriage Center

VISIT US ON THE WEB

Made in the USA
San Bernardino, CA
13 September 2015